FIFTY WAYS FOR THE FIFTY DAYS

**Creative Education Activities
for
Easter through Pentecost**

by
Phyllis Vos Wezeman
and
Jude Dennis Fournier

DEDICATIONS

To Donald W. Dilg, C.S.C.

...the Encourager. (PVW)

To Mary Jane Fedder, O.P.

...whose friendship is so precious to me. (JDF)

Illustrator: Ezequiel Lopez

FIFTY WAYS FOR THE FIFTY DAYS:
Creative Education Activities
for Easter through Pentecost

by Phyllis Vos Wezeman
and
Jude Dennis Fournier

Copyright © 1990
EDUCATIONAL MINISTRIES, INC.

ISBN 0-940754-83-5

EDUCATIONAL MINISTRIES, INC.
165 Plaza Drive
Prescott, AZ 86303-5549

TABLE OF CONTENTS

INTRODUCTION

Beginnings...

Easter is a time of new beginnings; a time to celebrate the newness of life in the Risen Christ. Jesus' resurrection marked a new beginning for all creation. He arose and broke the chains of death and won victory for life. Easter begins a new liturgical season which provides us fifty days to celebrate this new life. This celebrating takes place during the springtime when the earth is beginning its own cycle of new life.

Jesus appeared to the ones he loved and proclaimed the Glory of God in the beginning of his resurrected life. For one of the followers, Peter, it was a new beginning when he was reinstated.

The Great Commission meant new beginnings, too. Jesus assigned the disciples and sent them into the world to begin the proclamation of the Gospel's good news.

Jesus' Ascension marked the beginning of his glorious reign over heaven and earth; King of Kings and Lord of Lords. This also marked a new beginning for those who were left on earth as they had been entrusted with the continuation of Jesus' ministry.

Because all this took place, Jesus promised he would send his Spirit so his believers could be afire with his love. It was a new beginning for all God's people.

Fifty Ways for the Fifty Days: Creative Education Ideas for Easter through Pentecost is a valuable resource to help people of all ages, but especially children, celebrate and understand this most glorious season. The season of Easter is the most important time of year for all Christian people. Use the five themes and the fifty ideas in this text as a way to celebrate it.

OVERVIEW

The period of time from Easter Sunday through the Day of Pentecost is often referred to as the "Fifty Days." The five themes in this book, He Arose, He Appeared, He Assigned, He Ascended and We're Afire, are based on the significant stories and events, recorded in the Gospels, that took place during this fifty day period.

Within each of the five themes there are ten activities, making a total of fifty suggested methods, for sharing these stories. Participatory approaches, those which involve the learners in the story, are emphasized. Since people have a variety of learning styles, such as auditory, visual and kinesthetic, at least one art, banner/textile, creative writing, drama, music, puppetry and storytelling idea is included in each chapter. Cartoon, clown/mime, dance/movement, food, game and photography techniques are offered in several of the sections.

The material in **Fifty Ways for the Fifty Days** may be used in many ways. Pick activities from each theme that will supplement and enhance existing curriculum, or use one of the chapters each week during the fifty day season and develop a lesson incorporating the ideas. Adapt the suggestions to meet the needs of the students and the specific situation.

It is important to become familiar with the scripture passage and the story before presenting the activity. Be sure to let the students know why they are doing the activity by relating the scripture to the process.

The fifty ways included in this volume use common materials which are readily available. Some activities may require advance preparation.

Fifty Ways for the Fifty Days is a valuable resource for church school teachers, religious education directors, pastors, worship and education committees, vacation church school coordinators, Bible club leaders, parents and others.

HE AROSE:
THE STORY OF JESUS' RESURRECTION

Scripture Passages:
Matthew 28:1-7
Mark 16:1-8
Luke 24:1-8
John 20:1-8

MIRACULOUS MOBILE

Materials:

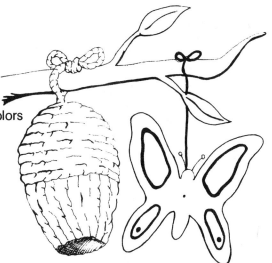

- Small tree branches
- Small round balloons
- Yarn or carpet thread in natural colors
- Glue
- Water
- Scissors
- White construction paper
- Crayons
- Black tempera paint
- Paint brushes
- Dishwashing liquid

Method:

Use the Miraculous Mobile to help the students understand the new life of Easter. The symbols of the cocoon and the butterfly can be used as parallels to the tomb and the resurrection of Jesus.

Begin the cocoon by passing out a balloon to each learner. Tell them to blow it up and to knot the end. Distribute paint brushes and glue that has been diluted with water. Use one part glue to two parts water. Instruct the pupils to cover the entire balloon with the mixture. Guide the children in layering the surface of the balloon with yarn or thread vertically and horizontally. Set the covered balloon aside and allow it to dry for twenty-four hours. Once it is dry, cut a round opening on one side of the cocoon. If desired, pull out the balloon. Tie a piece of yarn or thread to the top of the cocoon and set it aside.

Give a quarter sheet of white construction paper to each person and have them cut or draw a butterfly shape. Distribute crayons and tell the children to fill in the entire butterfly, both front and back, with a variety of colors. Provide paint and brushes and direct the group to cover both sides of the shape with black tempera that has been mixed with dishwashing liquid. Use one-quarter cup dishwashing liquid to one quart paint. Allow the butterfly to dry for five to eight minutes. Pass out scissors and show the "artists" how to use the point to gently scrape away some of the black so that the color of the butterfly will show through. Encourage the students to use lines and circles to make beautiful designs. Attach thread or yarn to the center of each butterfly for hanging.

Now put the Miraculous Mobiles together. Give each student a tree branch and have them tie the Easter symbols of the cocoon and the butterfly to it. Compare these to the tomb and resurrection of Jesus. Display the mobiles in the classroom, church, school or home.

SYMBOL STOLE

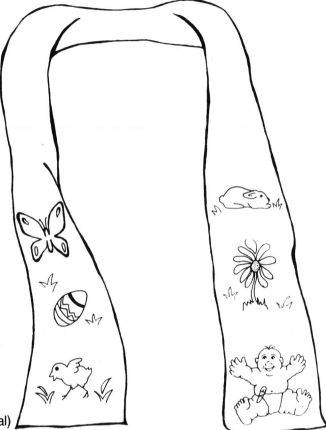

Materials:

- Felt
- Scissors
- Glue
- Markers
- Patterns (optional)
- Pictures of resurrection symbols from magazines, cards or posters

Method:

A Symbol Stole will help the students see and share a variety of Easter symbols. Explain that the stole is a sign that each person is called to ministry through the new life given by Jesus.

In advance, make a simple stole out of felt for each student. An alternative or additional project would be to make one stole to be used by the teacher or pastor.

Begin by showing pictures of Easter symbols. These could include signs of new life such as spring flowers, lilies, grass, eggs, baby animals, infants and butterflies. Ask the students to name other symbols. Have them pick several symbols to decorate their own stole or one to be used on the group stole.

Provide a variety of 4" x 4" felt squares. Patterns, prepared in advance, may be available for the students to use. Have them cut out the symbols they have chosen. Some may choose to decorate them with markers. Glue to the stole.

Give an opportunity to share the symbols and their personal meaning.

MYSTERY MANUSCRIPT

Materials:

- Paper
- Pencils
- 3" x 5" cards
- Box

Method:

Put the mystery of the Resurrection into words by doing a Mystery Manuscript. This creative writing project will allow the students to compose their own stories, poems, verses or passages based on the Easter story.

Brainstorm words associated with Easter, Resurrection and the Gospel Story. Choose ten or fifteen of these and write one word on each 3" x 5" card. Place them in the box. Distribute paper and pencils.

Pick five words from the box to be used in the Mystery Manuscript. Read the first word to the students and tell them to write one sentence or simple line expressing the first thought that comes to mind in hearing the word. The idea is not to define the word, but to express a feeling associated with it. Continue in this manner for the four remaining words.

Example:

Egg:
There's life inside.

Tomb:
It's empty and Jesus is gone.

Alleluia:
Our Easter song.

Angel:
Messenger of the good news.

Butterfly:
Beautiful new life.

Offer students the opportunity to share their Mystery Manuscripts with one other student or with the entire class.

GIVING GIFTS

Materials:

- Grocery bags
- Scissors
- Masking tape
- Markers
- Glue
- Construction paper
- **The Giving Tree** by
  Shel Silverstein (New York: Harper and Row, 1964)

Method:

The story of **The Giving Tree** and this activity will illustrate for the students that there can be new life even when death seems to be the end and there appears to be nothing else to give.

Read the book or tell the story to the students. Invite them to bring it to life by making props and acting it out.

Make a large tree out of split brown grocery bags or brown paper. This should be done in three parts: the stump, the trunk and the branches. Use construction paper to make apples and leaves. Glue the leaves to the branches, but tape on the apples for easy removal during the storytelling. Attach the three pieces of the tree to a wall or door.

Invite the students to play the various roles. Assign people to be the tree, the little boy, the older boy, the young man, the middle-aged man and the old man. In re-telling the story, have the tree give away its various gifts to each of the characters. Involve all the students by taking turns playing the people and doubling up on the roles. For example, have one student hold a basket while several others pick apples. Continue this procedure throughout the whole story until only the stump remains.

Allow time for sharing and talking about what the experience says to the students about the Easter story and Jesus' gift to them.

MUSICAL MESSAGES

Materials:

- Guitar or autoharp (if available)
- Music to "Michael, Row the Boat Ashore" or "Amazing Grace"

Method:

Music is an exciting way to tell the Easter story. The word "Alleluia," found in many songs, means "Praise the Lord." For a quick, easy song for all students to sing, use a familiar tune and make up new words that tell the Easter message.

Sing the word "Alleluia" to the tune Amazing Grace.

Write new words for the verses of "Michael, Row the Boat Ashore". Sing the Alleluia after each phrase. For example:

Jesus rose on Easter morn. Alleluia.
Jesus rose on Easter morn. Alleluia.
The angel said, "He lives again." Alleluia.
The angel said, "He lives again." Alleluia.
Mary went and told his friends. Alleluia.
Mary went and told his friends. Alleluia.
This new life brings joy to us. Alleluia.
This new life brings joy to us. Alleluia.

Other familiar songs to use could be "London Bridge is Falling Down" or "Go Tell Aunt Rody".

CARTON CREATIONS

Materials:

- Cardboard egg cartons
- Construction paper
- Scissors
- Glue
- Tempera paint
- Brushes
- Trims
- Pictures of baby bunnies and chicks.

Method:

Baby bunnies and chicks are a sign of new life and creating animal finger puppets is a fun way to illustrate this concept.

Show the pictures of the baby animals. Have each student choose to make the head of a bunny or a chick. Distribute egg carton cups and scissors. Carefully, cut a finger size hole in one side of the cup. The open end of the cup should be facing down. Pass out paint and brushes. Allow the students to paint the cup the color of their animal. Set it aside to dry. Cut features, such as ears, eyes, nose, mouth or whiskers, from construction paper and trims and glue in place.

As this project is being done, continue to illustrate and talk about the new life of Easter, Resurrection and Spring. Once the puppets are completed, encourage the students to use their Carton Creations to tell someone else about this new life.

SYMBOLIC STORIES

Materials:

- **The Very Hungry Caterpillar** by Eric Carle (New York: Philomel Books, 1983)
- Posterboard
- Scissors
- Markers

Method:

The popular children's book, **The Very Hungry Caterpillar**, illustrates the life cycle of a butterfly. In words and pictures it shows the transformation from caterpillar to cocoon to butterfly. It is readily available in many libraries or bookstores.

Read or tell the story to the students. Describe to them how this cycle can be compared to the life, death and resurrection of Jesus.

In advance, make posterboard props of the fruits and foods, as well as the caterpillar, cocoon and butterfly, to add a visual as well as an auditory dimension to the story.

For older students, read **Hope for the Flowers** by Trina Paulus (New York: Paulist Press, 1972).

CELEBRATION CLOWNS

Materials:

- Clown makeup in a variety of colors or watercolor paint trays
- Brushes
- Tissues

Method:

The symbolism of clowning lends itself well to the resurrection story. The clown is one who dies to self in order that someone else may have life. Around the world, the white face is the symbol of death. The colors which are put on the white face are symbols of new life. This new life, then, is shared with others through the gifts of dance, humorous skits, storytelling, silent movement and gesture which bring about laughter and joy.

Share the signs of new life through a face painting activity. Begin by brainstorming symbols such as hearts, butterflies, roses, other flowers, stars, balloons, etc. which might be used. Since the clown is one who gives, pair the students, have each person pick a symbol, and paint it on one another's faces.

Younger students may need assistance and a few volunteers may be helpful. If a clown from the congregation or community is available, his or her presence would further enhance the activity.

RAINBOW RIBBONS

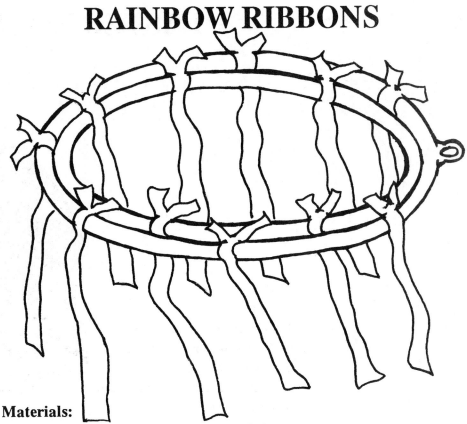

Materials:

- Embroidery hoops of various small sizes
- 1/4" or 1/2" ribbon in rainbow colors (2 yards per ribbon per student)
- Scissors
- Tape recorder
- Cassette tapes

Method:

Movement and dance are fun ways for students to express Easter joy. The rainbow colors, as well, are signs of God's promise to always love us. The Rainbow Ribbon hoops will aid and encourage children to freely participate in expressing joy in what Jesus has done for them. The hoops may be taken home as a reminder to continue praising God.

Construct the rainbow ribbon hoops by loosening the hoop pieces and running the various colors of ribbon through them at the bottom. Begin with red and insert it between the two hoops so that an even amount of ribbon hangs on each side. Continue for the remaining colors. Tighten the hoops and the ribbons will remain in place.

Play joyful music, such as the tapes **Tomorrow Is My Dancing Day** by Paul **Winter or Winter To Spring** by George Winston. These can be found in most music stores. Form a line and lead the students in a variety of movements. Encourage individual expression to show the excitement of the Easter story.

EASTER EGGS

Materials:

- Eggs
- Permanent markers or crayons
- Black liquid tempera paint
- Round toothpicks
- Diluted white glue or spray varnish
- Basket

Method:

The Easter egg is traditionally used as a symbol of new life. The shell is a reminder of Jesus' tomb and the inside contains the elements of life.

Ukranian eggs are displayed throughout the year as a constant reminder that we are an Easter people. Usually, raw eggs are decorated and, in time, the yolk and the white will evaporate. They are not to be refrigerated. This project may be done with hard boiled eggs which will avoid the possibility of the eggs breaking during the activity. These, however, will only last for a few weeks. It is recommended that hard boiled eggs be used for decoration and not for eating.

Distribute an egg to each student. Use permanent markers or crayons to color the entire surface. Paint the whole egg with the black tempera. Allow it to dry completely. While the eggs are drying, discuss some of the symbols that can be etched on the painted shell. Ukranian Easter eggs often contain triangles which mean air, fire and water, sun representing good fortune, trees for eternal youth and health, flowers meaning love and charity and a wavy, endless line which represents eternity. Dots and checkerboards are used to fill in borders. Once the egg is dry, distribute toothpicks and ask the students to create several of these beautiful and meaningful designs by gently scraping off some of the black tempera. To give the egg a gloss and also to prevent further tempera from being chipped off, seal it with spray varnish or brushed on diluted white glue.

Invite the students to show the uniqueness of their individual eggs and place all of them in a large basket for display during the class period or Easter season.

HE APPEARED:
THE STORIES OF
JESUS' APPEARANCES

TO THE WOMEN:

- Matthew 28:9,10
- Luke 24:9-11
- John 20:10-18

POWERFUL POETRY

Materials:

- Paper
- Pens or pencils

Method:

When Jesus appeared to the women after the Resurrection, they probably had a variety of feelings. They might have been amazed, anxious, joyful and curious. Explore some of these feelings with the children by using a form of poetry called Cinquain. Cinquain poetry consists of five lines. The formula for writing it is as follows:

Line One: A one word noun

Line Two: Two adjectives that describe the noun

Line Three: Three "-ing" words that describe the noun

Line Four: Four words that describe a feeling about the noun

Line Five: One word that is a synonym for the noun

Example One:

Women
Frightened, amazed
Trusting, caring, sharing
Spread the Good News
Believers

Example Two:

Jesus
Arisen, Alive
Loving, forgiving, willing
Our God and Lord
Savior

Begin by writing one together as a class. Form small groups of children and invite each to write a second Cinquain poem. Use the poems as prayers to continue celebrating the excitement of Jesus' appearance.

JOYFUL JOURNEY

Materials:

- Tape, background music
- Cassette player

Method:

Joyful Journey is a guided meditation that will allow the students to imagine what it would have been like to have been with the women when they met Jesus on Easter morning. This activity will enable the learners to surface some of the feelings that might have been present on the day of the Resurrection.

Put on a quiet, calm background music without words. Ask the students to close their eyes and to become aware of their own breathing. Read the meditation slowly, pausing after each sentence.

Guided Meditation:

In your mind's eye, we are going to take a walk. Imagine yourself walking out of this room to the outdoors. The day is Sunday and it is early morning. It is a beautiful Spring day. You are aware of the birds singing their morning songs. The blue sky is filled with white fluffy clouds floating happily overhead. You see that the trees are full of pink and white blossoms. The air is fragrant and clean, and a cool Spring breeze passes through your hair. Even as the sun shines warmly and the day is beautiful, you are sad. You can't forget that your friend Jesus is dead. Just two days earlier the soldiers nailed him to a cross. As you walk in the beauty of the garden, you are aware that your heart is broken.

You notice in the distance three people who look to be women. As they get closer, you are aware of the great joy and happiness expressed in their smiles and on their faces. They speak to you of your sadness on such a beautiful Spring day. You share with them the news of your friend, Jesus, and what has happened to Him. The women, in turn, tell you that Jesus is their friend as well, and that they saw Him earlier that morning. He is alive! The women tell you that Jesus told them to share this Good News with all those who loved Him. How do you feel knowing that Jesus is no longer dead? In your imagination, share with the women how you feel knowing that Jesus is alive and has risen. The women continue on their way leaving you to tell the news of the Resurrection to others.

As you begin your journey back to this room, think about what you will say to others when you see them. When you are ready, open your eyes and sit quietly. Now we are ready to share our journey.

After the meditation, encourage the children to speak of their experience. For example, ask:

What did the day look like?
Who were the women?
What did they say?
What feelings did you experience when they said Jesus was alive?
How would you tell others about it?

Guide the discussion and continue it as long as the children are contributing their ideas.

THE MEN ON THE ROAD TO EMMAUS:
- Luke 24:13-35

DRAMATIC DISCOVERY

Materials:
- Bible
- Scripts
- Costume pieces

Method:

The two men on the road to Emmaus made a dramatic discovery. They realized that their traveling companion had been the risen Savior. Help the students experience this story through the use of drama. Create an easy script by breaking the scripture passage into character parts. A sample script, based on Luke 24:13-35, is provided.

Take turns having the children play the four parts: the narrator, Jesus, Cleopas and the unnamed man. Drape strips of fabric over the students' heads and shoulders to create simple costumes.

Sample Script:

Narrator: Now that same day two of them were going to a village called Emmaus, about seven miles from Jerusalem. They were talking with each other about everything that had happened. As they talked and discussed these things with each other, Jesus himself came up and walked along with them; but they were kept from recognizing him.

Jesus: What are you discussing together as you walk along?

Cleopas: Are you the only one living in Jerusalem who doesn't know the things that have happened there in these days?

Jesus: What things?

Cleopas: About Jesus of Nazareth. He was a prophet, powerful in word and deed before God and all the people. The chief priest and our rulers handed him over to be sentenced to death, and they crucified him; but we had hoped that he was the one who was going to redeem Israel.

Man: And what is more, it is the third day since all this took place. In addition, some of our women amazed us. They went to the tomb early this morning but didn't find his body. They came and told us that they had seen a vision of angels, who said he was alive. Then some of our companions went to the tomb and found it just as the women had said, but him they did not see.

Jesus: How foolish you are, and how slow of heart to believe all that the prophets have spoken! Did not the Christ have to suffer these things and then enter his glory?

Narrator: And beginning with Moses and all the Prophets, he explained to them what was said in all the Scriptures concerning himself.

As they approached the village to which they were going, Jesus acted as if he were going farther. They urged him strongly:

Cleopas: Stay with us, for it is nearly evening; the day is almost over.

Narrator: So he went in to stay with them.

When he was at the table with them, he took bread, gave thanks, broke it and began to give it to them. Then their eyes were opened and they recognized him, and he disappeared from their sight. They asked each other:

Cleopas: Were not our hearts burning within us while he talked with us on the road and opened the Scriptures to us?

Narrator: They got up and returned at once to Jerusalem. There they found the Eleven and those with them, assembled together and saying, "It is true! The Lord has risen and has appeared to Simon." Then the two told what had happened on the way, and how Jesus was recognized by them when he broke the bread.

PIECE PUZZLE

Materials:

- Yellow, white, brown and tan construction paper or posterboard
- Scissors
- Markers
- Tape
- Basket

Method:

The two men on the road to Emmaus didn't have a clue that their traveling companion was Jesus until he broke bread with them. Recall the story of the Last Supper for the children. Remind them that it was on this occasion that Jesus broke bread, shared it with his disciples and asked them to always remember him. Help the children realize the significance of both of these stories through the use of this Piece Puzzle activity.

Prepare five loaves of bread from construction paper or posterboard. Use a variety of shapes and colors. On the back of each loaf, write one of the following words: Jesus, Is, Our, Risen, Savior. Cut each individual loaf into puzzle pieces. Keep each puzzle separate.

Divide the class into five groups. Distribute a puzzle to each group and instruct them to put it together. Once each puzzle is completed, guide the students in discovering the hidden message that appears when the words on the backs of the five loaves are combined. Invite each group to say the word that has been formed by their puzzle. Challenge the students to put the five words together to form an Easter message. Answers might be Jesus Is Our Risen Savior, Jesus Our Savior Is Risen or Our Risen Savior Is Jesus.

Tape each puzzle together and place the five loaves into a basket which can be displayed in the classroom.

TO THE DISCIPLES:
- Luke 24:36-49
- John 20:19-23

FLANNELGRAPH FOLLOWERS

Materials:
- Pellon
- Scissors
- Markers
- Patterns
- Cardboard or thin plywood
- Background material such as felt, corduroy or indoor/outdoor carpeting

Method:

Jesus' appearance to the disciples calmed their fears and confirmed to them that He was truly alive. Make the story come alive for the students by inviting them to take part in the Flannelgraph Followers activity. Tell the children that each of them will make a figure which represents one of the followers of Jesus. Begin by having the students name some of the apostles and have each person choose one that they will make.

If patterns are to be used, prepare them by cutting people from used Sunday School papers or religious coloring books. Cover the cardboard or plywood with the felt, corduroy or carpeting.

Pass out a pattern to each student, together with a piece of pellon and a marker. Instruct them to draw or trace the person they have chosen. Provide additional markers for coloring and highlighting the pellon piece. The Jesus figure should be made by the teacher.

Lead the children in re-telling the story of Jesus' appearance to the disciples. Have the students take turns placing their piece in the scene.

Discuss with the students ways that they, too, are followers of Jesus. Include things like helping someone with a school project, bringing a meal to a shut-in or going to Sunday School. Send the flannelgraph piece home with each student as a reminder to continue to be Jesus' follower.

TO THOMAS:
- John 20:24

BELIEVERS BANNER

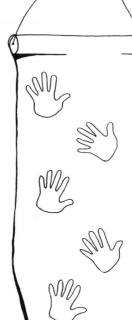

Materials:
- Cloth
- Dowel or metal rod
- Felt or fabric pieces
- Permanent markers
- Scissors
- Glue

Method:

Thomas was not with the disciples when Jesus appeared to them the first time, so he doubted that Jesus was really alive. It was not until he was invited to physically reach out his hand and place it into the marks on Jesus' hands and side that he believed.

Brainstorm with the students the various ways that they recognize Jesus in others and how others recognize Jesus in them. Suggest things like being filled with joy, showing compassion for others, using a special gift or talent and reaching out in friendship to someone in need. Tell the students that they will be making a group banner to illustrate these ideas.

Prepare the banner background in advance. On the top of the banner write with permanent markers or attach felt letters to form the words: "My Lord and My God". Provide an opportunity for each student to trace his or her hand on a piece of felt or fabric and cut it out. Ask them to write their name in the palm of the hand. On each finger have them write a way people see Jesus in them. Refer to the brainstormed list for ideas. Glue the hands to the banner background. Insert the dowel or metal rod and find an appropriate place to hang it.

AT THE SEASHORE:
● John 21:1-11

SHADOW STORY

Materials:
- Construction paper or posterboard
- Scissors
- Cellophane
- Ribbon
- Flexible straws
- Tape
- Paper punches
- White bed sheet
- Rope
- Clothespins
- Light source

Method:

Jesus' power was again displayed to the disciples when he appeared to them at the seashore. The story of the miraculous catch of fish illustrates this well. Excite the children about this story through the use of a shadow puppet play.

Direct the students in the construction of shadow puppet fish. Each person will begin by making one. Additional fish may be created if time allows. Distribute construction paper or posterboard and scissors to each person. Paper of various abstract shapes will trigger imagination and help the learners create unique fish. Have each student cut out a large fish. Place the paper punch, cellophane, tape and ribbon within sharing distance of the "puppeteers." Show them how to cut or punch designs, such as scales and fins, into it. Demonstrate taping colored cellophane behind the cut-outs. Ribbons can be added for tails. Allow time for the children to decorate their shadow puppets.

Pass out a straw to each person. Model how to attach it to the fish. Bend the straw and tape the smaller portion to the center back of the fish. Use the rest of the straw as the handle by which the fish is moved. Guide the group as they attach their straws to their puppets.

In advance, hang the white sheet from the rope. This should be placed in a large open area of the room so students can move easily in front and in back of it. Place the light source behind the sheet.

Ask the students to sit in front of the sheet. Take turns having the children try out their shadow puppet fish behind the screen. Also exchange fish so that each person may see his or her own behind the sheet. To demonstrate the many fish in the miraculous catch, line up the students and continue adding more fish, one at a time, until all the students are back stage and all the fish are in the scene.

Send the fish home with each student.

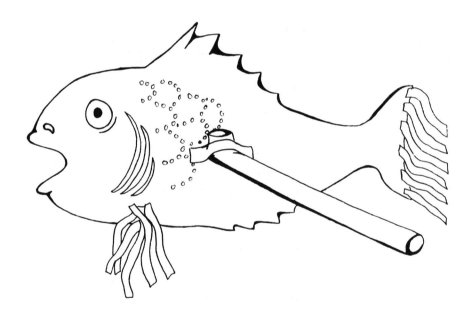

BREAKING BREAD

Materials:

- 1 1/2 cups warm water
- 2 packages yeast
- 1 teaspoon salt
- 1 Tablespoon sugar
- 4 cups flour
- 2 eggs, beaten
- Kosher salt
- Mixing bowl
- Utensils
- Floured board
- Cookie sheets
- Oven

Method:

This simple bread recipe and activity will give the students an opportunity to bake bread and break it together like Jesus did with the disciples at the seashore.

The soft pretzel is made in the form of arms crossed in prayer which symbolize the love that we have for God and for one another.

Follow this recipe:

Place the water in the mixing bowl. Sprinkle the yeast over it and wait until the yeast is wet. Add sugar, salt and flour. Stir dough until soft, dry and crumbly. Knead on floured board until smooth. Take a ball of dough about the size of a walnut and make a "snake." Then fold it into a pretzel. Paint with beaten egg and sprinkle with kosher salt. Bake on greased cookie sheet at 425 degrees about fifteen to twenty minutes, depending on the size of the pretzels. Eat while warm.

TO PETER:
- John 21:15-19

SHEPHERD'S STORY

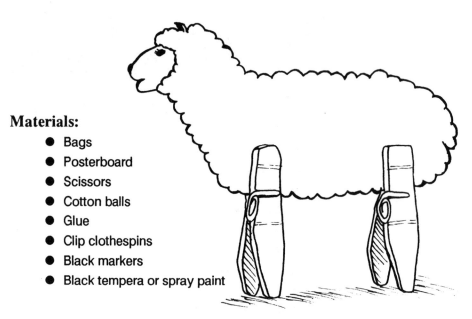

Materials:
- Bags
- Posterboard
- Scissors
- Cotton balls
- Glue
- Clip clothespins
- Black markers
- Black tempera or spray paint

Method:

Three times Jesus asked Peter if he loved him. With each of Peter's positive replies Jesus entrusted him with the task of feeding His sheep. Explain to the students that although this is a question Jesus asked Peter a long time ago, he also asks it of us today. This activity will remind the children that they too are Jesus' sheep as well as His shepherds.

Read or tell the story found in John 21:15-19. Each time the interaction between Jesus and Peter is completed, give each child a small bag containing part of a sheep. The first bag should contain the posterboard body shape, the second the cotton balls and the third two clip clothespins. Once the third question is asked and the third bag is given, each child will have the parts needed to construct a sheep.

Distribute black markers and begin by drawing a face on the posterboard form. Glue cotton balls to the remainder of the shape. Paint the clip clothespins black and once they are dry, attach them to the bottom of the sheep. The clothespins may be painted in advance.

Place all the sheep together on a table and remind the children that we are all part of Jesus' flock. He is our shepherd and He invites us to shepherd one another.

32

LOVE LESSONS

Materials:

- Newsprint
- Markers

Method:

Mime is a way of communicating without words. Lead the students in a series of exercises that will help them express messages of love for others and for God.

Brainstorm ways to show love to another person and to God. Write these on a blackboard or newsprint so they are visible to the students. Have each pupil choose one way that he or she will mime for the group. Invite the other children to guess the action that is being portrayed. Continue until everyone has had a turn.

HE ASSIGNED:
THE STORY OF
THE GREAT COMMISSION

Scripture Passage: Matthew 28:16-20

COMMISSIONED CUT-OUTS

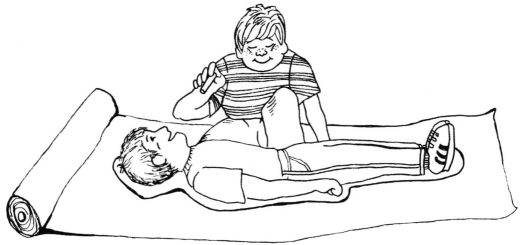

Materials:

- Butcher paper
- Pencils
- Scissors
- Markers

Method:

The words of the Great Commission, "Go and make disciples of all nations, baptizing them in the name of the Father and of the Son and of the Holy Spirit, and teaching them to obey everything I have commanded you," were spoken thousands of years ago. They were heard by the faithful followers of Jesus, the disciples, and intended as a challenge to them to carry on Jesus' ministry on earth while he was in heaven. The words of Matthew 28:19-20 still speak to the faith-filled followers of Jesus today. This activity will give the participants an opportunity to reflect on ways that Jesus continues to commission his current disciples. It will help the children realize that being a Christian means acting in special ways to spread the Savior's story.

Invite the learners to brainstorm ways their lives show that they are Christians. Encourage them to name ways that they feel commissioned and called to share Jesus' love. Some examples may be doing yard work for the elderly, taking part in a hunger walk, visiting the sick, and doing extra tasks for the family.

Ask the students to make large body tracings to illustrate what they have been discussing. Cut a piece of butcher paper the length of each child. Pair the students, distribute pencils or markers, and instruct the partners to take turns tracing one another onto the paper. Tell each person to cut out his or her outline. Invite the children to use the markers to fill in the tracings by writing or drawing things they do for others that show that they, too, have been commissioned by Jesus.

Hang the completed tracings around the room. Allow the students to share and describe their work.

COMMUNICATIVE CLOTHING

Materials:

- T-shirts
- Fabric crayons
- Paper
- Pencils
- Iron
- Ironing board
- Brown paper

Method:

Jesus entrusted the disciples with the task of being his servants. He told them to preach and teach and baptize in his name. This message was spread with words and actions, as well as non-verbally. Today people often wear clothing that contains words or symbols which communicate powerful Christian messages. This activity provides instructions for making t-shirts with not only a word but also a symbol to help the students communicate that they, too, are servants of Christ.

Pass out a piece of paper and pencil to each person. Instruct them to write "servant" on it, backwards. Be sure all the letters are written in reverse. Tell the children to design the "t" of the word to look like a cross. Provide fabric crayons and give the pupils an opportunity to color their designs. Suggest that the letters be colored with solid, steady strokes and that each letter be outlined in black.

The next step of the project should be carefully supervised by one or several adults. Set up the ironing board and pre-heat the iron to a very high setting. As the students finish coloring, invite one person at a time to bring his or her t-shirt to the ironing station. Position the front of the shirt over the board and place the colored paper face-down on it. Cover the design with brown paper. Iron the design into the fabric using a slow, firm, steady motion. The iron must be very hot for the design to transfer properly. Carefully remove the papers from the shirt. As the designs are being transferred, use the time to talk with each student about what it means to be a servant who has been entrusted with spreading the good news of Jesus' love. Remind them that this can be done at home, school and church as well as in many other places.

SHARED STORY

Materials:

- Construction paper
- Crayons
- Markers
- Scissors
- Paper punch
- Ribbon or yarn

Method:

The apostles were assigned to go two by two and continue the work of Jesus. They travelled from land to land healing the sick and teaching the good news of the gospel message. This creative writing activity can be used to help the students think about ways in which they can share Jesus' love and make a difference in the world. The individual pages of the project will be combined to make a class book.

Before the students arrive, cut the construction paper into the shape of a globe. Distribute a piece to each person. Make the cover page with the class by writing the words "We share God's love with the world by..." on it. Ask the students to write several sentences, a story or a poem to complete the statement on their own book page. Provide markers and crayons and invite them to illustrate this message.

When the pages are finished, collect them and bind them into one book. Punch holes into the side of the pages and tie them together with a length of yarn.

A variation of this project could be to cut the paper into the shape of a hand. Invite the students to write a poem describing ways in which they could use their hands for purposes of healing. For example, they could offer a handshake in friendship or in welcome, help a friend who has fallen down, or bring a gift to a shut-in.

DISCIPLE DRAMAS

Materials:

- Bible
- Costumes or costume pieces
- Props, optional

Method:

When the apostles were assigned and commissioned to carry on the work of Jesus they must have been filled with a deep sense of responsibility and fear. To continue the work that Jesus started was a challenging task. It is still a challenging task for people today. This activity will enable the participants to dramatize some of the thoughts and feelings the disciples must have experienced as they stood on the hillside with Jesus. It will also help them explore some of the feelings they have about sharing the Gospel with others.

Begin by reading the story of the Great Commission, Matthew 28:16-20, to the group. Ask the children to name some of the feelings the disciples may have experienced. These could be joy, fear, anticipation, hesitation, eagerness and many others. Invite each person to become one of the apostles and to present a first person drama. Encourage the "actors" to speak in the present tense and to share the feelings of what it might have been like to be asked to carry out this incredible work. If props and costumes are available, use them to enhance the presentations.

MUSICAL MESSAGE

Materials:

● Music, "Jesus Loves the Little Children"

Method:

"Jesus Loves the Little Children" is a familiar song which emphasizes the message of the Great Commission. It can be sung with the children and also used to lead them in a guided or directed prayer.

Ask the group to sing the first verse together. Invite them to participate in a prayer in which they can remember children in all parts of the world. Sing the first two lines of the song again. Stop after the phrase "All the children of the world." Explain that each continent will be named and that a brief pause will follow each statement. Encourage the group to pray for the people of that particular region during the silence. Suggest that they remember their physical and spiritual needs.

Name each continent and pause briefly after each of them. After the prayer, sing the remainder of the song and conclude with "Amen."

SINGING SONGS

Materials:

Music to songs such as:

"He's Got the Whole World in His Hands"
"It's A Small World"
"We Are the World"
"What the World Needs Now"
"Love in any Language"
"For God So Loved the World"

Method:

Jesus' great commission included people throughout the entire world. There are many songs associated with a world theme. Share some of them with the participants. Hold an Easter season sing-a-long during a portion of the class, or play the music on records, tapes or CD's.

PUPPET POPULATION

Materials:

- Styrofoam cups
- Markers, permanent
- Yarn, fiberfill or fake fur
- Scissors
- Glue
- Fabric
- Trims
- Resource materials

Method:

Jesus commanded the disciples to go into all the world and preach the Gospel. Puppets can acquaint the participants with people and places throughout the earth and introduce them to various countries and cultures. A basic material, a cup, can be used to construct interesting, individualized puppet creations.

Begin by providing resources including encyclopedias, magazines, travel brochures and maps, on various populations and locations. After reviewing these materials ask each person to select a country and to make a puppet to represent it.

Distribute a cup to each pupil. Place the remaining supplies within sharing distance of the students. Tell the group that the cups will become the puppet heads. Instruct them to turn the cups up-side-down, so the bottom of the cup becomes the top of the head. Demonstrate how to use permanent markers to draw a face on one side of the cup. Direct the learners to draw faces on their cups.

Make hair from yarn, fiberfill or fake fur and glue it to the top of the heads. Cut a piece of fabric to fit around the opening of the cup. Glue the top edge of the fabric to the bottom of the rim. Allow time for each child to complete his or her puppet in this manner.

Give each student an opportunity to "introduce" his or her puppet and to find its country on a map.

SYNCOPATED STORY

Materials:

- Rhythm story

Method:

When Jesus gave his disciples the Great Commission he invited them to participate in spreading his love to people throughout the world. Use the Syncopated Story as a way to involve the learners and to inspire them to be Jesus' modern day disciples and continue spreading the Good News to people everywhere.

In a Syncopated Story the message is told by clapping a rhythm and echoing a rhyme. The leader says a line and participants repeat it back. Begin by establishing the clapping pattern, one clap on the knees and one clap of the hands. Practice it several times. Chant the first line of the story to this rhythm and tell the group to echo it back. Communicate the entire message in the manner. Maintain the established rhythm throughout the activity.

Story:

They were gathered on a hillside
On a very special day.
Jesus gave a great commission,
He had special words to say:

"I am going back to heaven,
but there's work on earth to do.
You're my friends and my disciples.
I'm entrusting it to you.

I have power on earth and heaven,
and I'm telling you to go.
To people everywhere on earth
My love and care to show.

Teach them all the things I've told you.
Baptize them into the name
Of the Father, Son and Spirit.
Tell the reason why I came.

Even though I'll be far from you,
Lo, I'll always be with you.
And my very special blessing
Will be on everything you do.

FOLLOWER'S FEET

Materials:

- White bedsheet
- Masking or duct tape
- Tempra paint, variety of colors
- Dishpans
- Water
- Liquid soap
- Towels

Method:

After the disciples were commissioned, they journeyed near and far sharing the love and hope that Jesus gave them. People today continue to be filled with Easter hope and this calls them to journey with a special purpose. The Follower's Feet activity can help the children understand this concept in a fun and festive way.

Spread the bedsheet in the center of a large room. Tape the corners and the sides to the floor. Pour each color of tempra paint into a separate dishpan. Add a small amount of liquid soap to the tempra. This will aid clean-up at the conclusion of the activity. Place the dishpans of paint around the sides of the sheet.

Invite the children to remove their shoes and socks. Instruct one or two students at a time to choose a color and to carefully step into the dishpan containing it. Direct each person to slowly walk across the sheet. Provide wet paper towels at the end of the walk and assist with clean-up. Continue this procedure until everyone has had a turn.

When the activity is completed talk about the way the feet seem to be going in different directions, yet they all symbolize following Jesus. Also note that when one color touches another, a change takes place. Comment that when Jesus touches people's lives they become very special and different. Ask the learners to name examples. Some may be:

people act in more loving ways
people help others in need
people treat others with respect

Cut or draw letters to form the words "Follower's Feet" and place them on the top of the banner to show that the commissioning journey is still taking place today. Hang the completed banner in a prominent location for all to see.

POWERFUL PICTURES

Materials:

- Camera
- Film
- Bulletin Board
- Tacks

Method:

Congregations and Christian community groups are carrying out the Great Commission in many ways today. This activity will help the children identify some of them. Concrete examples might include the work of soup kitchens, community centers, nursing homes, hospitals, day care facilities and homeless shelters.

Arrange a field trip to one or several of these sites. Bring a camera and, after asking permission, photograph ways in which the news of Jesus' love is being spread.

After the visit, involve the students in using the pictures to make a bulletin board collage. Display it in the classroom or church to illustrate the Great Commission in action.

If the equipment is available, a video or slide show may be made instead.

HE ASCENDED:
THE STORY OF JESUS' ASCENSION

Scripture Passages:
Mark 16:19
Luke 24:50, 51
Acts 1:9-12

DRAMATIC DAY

Materials:

- Balloons, round (one per two children)
- Newspaper strips
- Wallpaper paste
- Plastic basins
- Water
- Posterpaints
- Brushes
- Scissors

Method:

The disciples, and possibly other followers, were present when Jesus ascended into heaven. This was a dramatic day. Each person who watched the event must have told the story to many people. Each witness probably described the account using different details. This activity will give the participants an opportunity to pretend to be eye-witnesses of the Ascension and to dramatize the event with the use of masks and first-person stories.

Read the account of the Ascension to the learners. Ask each person to think about one of the people who saw Jesus being taken into heaven. Inform the group that this person could be a man, woman, teenager or child. He or she could be a disciple, or a traveller passing by as the event took place. Tell the students that they will work in pairs to make masks representing these people. Assign partners.

Demonstrate the mask-making process to the group. Begin by blowing up a balloon and knotting the end. Combine the wallpaper paste and water according to the package directions and place the mixture in a plastic basin. Dip a strip of newspaper into the paste. Squeeze the excess mixture from the paper by pulling it through the fingers as it is removed from the basin. Place the strip on the balloon. Continue this process until four to five layers of newspaper have been placed on the surface of the balloon.

Provide supplies and allow time for the students to complete the process. Let the balloons dry for twenty-four hours before proceeding with the project.

The next step is to cut the balloon in half lengthwise. Guide the students as they use scissors to complete this procedure. Tell them to pull the balloon away from the hardened paper and to discard the rubber pieces. Tell each partner to take a half to use for the activity. Instruct the children to carefully cut two eyes and a mouth out of the masks.

Make posterpaints and brushes available and allow the students to paint the masks to represent the character they chose.

Take turns letting the children use their masks to relate first person accounts of the Ascension story.

MESSAGE MARKERS

Materials:

- White felt
- Rainbow ribbon
- Scissors
- Glue
- Markers
- Alphabet pasta
- Food coloring
- Paper towels
- Containers

Method:

Two significant symbols are combined in the Message Markers activity to help the children reflect on the ways God keeps His promises. A cloud made from felt and a rainbow made from ribbon are joined to create a bookmark. The rainbow represents God's promise to never again destroy the world with a flood and also His promise to always love His people. The person of Christ, the ascended Lord, shows us that God's love is constant and confirms God's faithfulness in keeping His promises. The cloud, a symbol associated with the Ascension, serves as a reminder that there are also many promises connected with this event. Jesus promised the disciples that he would send the Holy Spirit and this was fulfilled at Pentecost. Jesus also promised his believers that he would go to prepare a place for them and that some day he would come again and take them to be with him forever. Emphasize these promises to the learners as the parts of the bookmark are being made and assembled.

If desired, draw a pattern for a cloud and duplicate it for the children. Distribute a piece of white felt and a pair of scissors to each youth. Instruct them to cut two identical cloud shapes. Give each person a five inch length of ribbon. Tell the group to glue the top one inch of the ribbon to the bottom edge of one of the clouds. Show the students how to place the second cloud shape on top and glue the pieces together.

Invite the pupils to place their names on the clouds to signify in a personal way that these promises have been given to them. The names may be written on the clouds in permanent markers. Alphabet pasta may also be used. Provide bowls of the pasta and allow the children to find the letters of their names in the noodles. Guide the young people as they glue the letters to one or both sides of their clouds. The letters may be colored with marker. They may also be colored by soaking them in food coloring in advance. If this method is used, the pieces should be drained thoroughly on paper towels before they are given to the youngsters.

Remind the children that they also bear the name Christian and reflect with them on ways in which they live up to this name.

Suggest that the students use the bookmarks to designate the story of the Ascension in their Bibles.

MAJESTIC MESSAGES

Materials:

- Fabric, cotton muslin
- Scissors
- Permanent markers or fabric paints
- Sewing machine

Method:

Mark's account of the Ascension includes the phrase, "He (Jesus) was taken up to heaven and sat at the right side of God." The phrase right side, or right hand, denotes a position of honor and majesty. Jesus is the one through whom God the Father administers the universe and everyone in it. In thinking about this segment of the story, a banner making activity will help the children discover dimensions of Jesus' royalty.

Talk with the children about the concept of royalty. Ask them to reflect on the words and images that come to mind as they think about this theme. Some obvious answers might be a crown, robe, scepter, people and world.

Read Mark 16:19 to the group and talk with them about the phrase "right hand/side of God." Help them understand that this indicates the position of royalty God gave to Jesus. Ask if the same images can be associated with this scripture passage.

Provide a cloth square for each person. Pass out permanent markers or fabric paints and tell the girls and boys to draw a picture on the material to depict Jesus' royalty and majesty. Suggest that their symbols or designs be large enough to touch the four sides of the square.

When the squares have been completed, collect the pieces and sew them together to make a banner, wall hanging or table covering. Display it as a reminder, for the children and for others who see it, of Jesus' royalty and majesty.

ADVOCATE ACROSTICS

Materials:

- Paper
- Pencils or markers

Method:

Advocate Acrostics is a creative writing activity intended to help the children not only understand the role of an advocate, but also comprehend that Jesus fulfills this role for them in a special way in heaven.

Since some of the youngsters may be unfamiliar with the term "advocate," begin by showing or sharing examples to explain it. An advocate is someone who pleads the case of another person. Show pictures or talk about a trial in which an attorney is pleading the case of his or her client. Another example could be a teacher who is explaining a situation to the principal on behalf of a student.

Tell the group that Jesus is our Advocate in the presence of his Father in heaven. Emphasize to the children that knowing Jesus is in heaven praying for them should be a source of comfort and strength for them as Christians. Ask the students to talk about the feelings associated with the assurance that Jesus is their constant, compassionate Advocate. Answers may include the words happy, relieved, safe and trusting.

Make the activity very personal for the students by inviting them to write a type of poetry called an Acrostic. Distribute paper and pencils or markers to each person. If desired, the poems may be written on colored paper which has been or could be cut into interesting shapes.

Tell each person to write his or her name vertically down the left side of the paper. Explain that for each letter of their name they will be writing a word, beginning with that letter, to describe how they feel knowing that a benefit of the Ascension is that Jesus is in heaven acting as their advocate. For example, for the name Charles, the acrostic might read:

C onfident
H appy
A ffirmed
R elaxed
L oved
E nabled
S afe

Provide time for each person to prepare his or her poem. When the task is completed, invite individuals to read their work. The creative writing projects may be displayed on a bulletin board, or they may be included in an issue of a church newsletter.

BALLOON BOUQUETS

Materials:

- Balloons (three per child)
- Helium, if available
- String or sticks
- Markers, permanent

Method:

Ascension Day is a time for celebration. During festive occasions, balloons are often used to create a sense of joy and happiness. This activity not only uses balloons as bright and beautiful decorations, it also incorporates a creative writing dimension on them.

It is important to note that balloons should be used in a way which does not harm the environment. Balloon launches are strongly discouraged as environmentalists point out that many animals choke on the broken pieces which become scattered across the earth.

In advance, prepare three balloons for each child. If helium is available, use it to inflate the balloons. Tie a piece of string onto each of them. If helium is not available, blow up the balloons and attach them to sticks.

As a way to celebrate Jesus' Ascension, pass out a Balloon Bouquet and a permanent marker to each participant. Tell the group that a word is to be written on each balloon. Instruct them to write the word "Jesus" on one, "Is" on a second and to choose a word to print on the third. The third word should complete the sentence. For example, it could be "Lord," "King," "Ruler" or "Alive."

The three word sentences may easily be turned into a type of poetry called a quick couplet. The first line of the poem may be written on one side of the balloon, and the concluding line may be printed on the other. Some examples include:

Jesus is Lord.
He's adored.

Jesus is King.
Let us sing.

To heaven's King,
Praise I'll bring.

Use the balloons to enhance a worship or church school space, or as bright and beautiful decorations at a church social hour or dinner.

JOYFUL GESTURES

Materials:

- 1 cup Joy dishwashing liquid
- 3 T. vodka
- 10 cups water
- Container(s)
- Wands
- Music
    * And the Father Will Dance
      Rev. Carey Landry
    * Rejoice, the Lord is King
    * Rejoice in the Lord Always

Method:

After Jesus had spoken to the disciples and assured them that the Holy Spirit would come to empower them to be his witnesses, he was taken up into heaven. As the faithful followers watched, a cloud received Jesus out of their sight. It may have been a time of sadness for those who were left behind and yet it was also a time of joy as Jesus returned to heaven, and to his father, to establish his reign over all the earth. This activity will enable the children to participate in a time of creative play to celebrate Jesus' Ascension and to enjoy the air, clouds and sky which were important elements of the event.

Take the group outside, preferably to a large open space or field. Comment on the beauty of the clouds and the sky. Invite the youngsters to breathe deeply and to be filled with the fresh air. If the Ascension story has not previously been told, share it with the group at this time.

Invite the pupils to celebrate Jesus' Ascension. Put on music and encourage them to move freely about the space. In advance, prepare or purchase bubble stuff. Joy brand dishwashing detergent works best and the addition of vodka gives the bubbles a stiffer consistency which makes them last longer. Make containers of the solution and wands available for the students to use. Suggest that the boys and girls watch the bubbles as they ascend into the air and that they imagine what it would have been like to have been one of the disciples who watched the Lord ascend into heaven.

Gather the children in a circle and conclude with a time of prayer.

SERVANTS OF THE SAVIOR

Materials:
- Paper lunch bags
- Newspaper
- Paper towel tubes
- Rubber bands or string
- Markers
- Yarn
- Fabric
- Scissors

Method:

As the ascended Lord, Jesus Christ rules in heaven as the head of the Church. On earth, the message and mission of the church is carried out by its members throughout the world. This puppetry activity will help the children understand that they are called to do Jesus' work on earth. It will also help them identify ways in which this is accomplished.

Invite each person to make a puppet representing him or her self. Pass out a bag and a tube to each person. Place the remaining materials within reach of the students. Tell the children to loosely crumple two or three sheets of newspaper and to place them in the bag. Instruct them to insert the paper towel tube into the center of the bag. Demonstrate how to gather the bag around the tube and to secure it with a rubber band or a piece of string. Using the markers, guide the young people as they draw their own faces on the bags.

Hair made from yarn and costumes cut from fabric may be added to the puppets, if desired. Show the pupils how to hold the puppets by the tubes in order to operate them.

Working individually or as partners, encourage the pupils to use their puppets to act out ways they minister in Jesus' name in the church today. Suggest areas of service as well as ways to glorify and praise God. Provide an opportunity for each pupil to share an example with the entire group.

PAINTED PICTURES

Materials:

- Construction paper (green, blue, purple, brown, assorted colors)
- Watercolor paints
- Brushes
- Containers
- Water
- Stapler
- Staples

Method:

As the scripture passage describing the Ascension is read or told, people hearing it may form mental images to illustrate the scenes of the story. Various colors might be associated with these pictures. Two of the most obvious color connections are the blue sky and the white clouds. The Painted Pictures activity is intended to provide students with the experience of creating a color story to use to review and remember this important event.

Tell the story of the Ascension to the group and ask them to visualize the scenes described by the words. Invite the listeners to name some of the colors that they saw in their mental pictures. Tell them that they will have the opportunity to make a special book of colors to help them remember the story.

Set the paint supplies at convenient intervals on the tables being used for the activity. Invite the students to gather around them.

Distribute a piece of green construction paper to each person and invite him or her to paint a picture of Jesus and the disciples on the hillside. Set the pages aside to dry.

Pass out sheets of blue construction paper and suggest that the learners paint a picture of Jesus ascending into heaven.

Use a variety of colors for the third page. It symbolizes the feelings of the disciples and other followers as they watched Jesus rise out of their sight. Allow the pupils to select their own color of paper to represent the emotions of one of the witnesses. Encourage the children to use the paint to illustrate this feeling on the paper.

Give out pieces of purple and suggest that the learners paint something which illustrates Jesus' royalty. This might be a symbol, such as a crown or scepter, commonly associated with the concept.

For the final color, pass out brown paper. Ask the students if they know what this represents. Be sure they understand that it stands for the earth. Encourage the artists to paint a picture of themselves doing something that carries out Jesus' work on earth.

After the pages are dry, have the children put them together in the proper sequence. Help them staple the left sides of the books together.

Suggest that the young people read their books to a family member or friend.

WORDS OF WONDER

```
        P  R  U  P  K  R  E  B  C  X  B  N  U  I  H
        U  E  Q  C  N  Q  P  R  F  O  E  S  W  C  J
        V  T  P  L  E  S  S  V  U  V  I  C  R  F  S
        V  U  P  X  H  E  O  V  A  O  U  U  F  M  F
        X  R  F  B  C  L  X  E  F  E  H  G  Q  P  Q
```
DISCIPLES
```
        M  N  R  Q  V  P  H  G  A  C  R  U  L  E  G
```
CLOUDS
```
        C  V  P  B  T  I  W  B  T  S  U  C  P  N  F
```
RETURN
```
        D  Q  L  H  F  C  J  K  H  I  Y  O  I  O  W
```
HEAVEN
```
        J  E  E  G  X  S  J  A  E  G  F  K  X  H  F
```
FATHER
```
        Z  X  W  H  X  I  L  E  R  H  V  E  S  R  R
```
CHURCH
```
        V  U  B  W  G  D  Y  T  S  T  T  O  B  T  X
```
JESUS
```
        J  C  L  O  U  D  S  Q  L  U  J  P  T  N  J
```
SIGHT
```
        S  A  X  J  G  L  K  B  A  S  S  Y  X  W  Y
```
KING
```
        G  N  A  J  C  M  Q  S  P  I  E  L  J  V  J
```
RULE
```
        J  V  L  D  B  R  K  Y  E  J  B  C  T  D  F
```

Materials:
- Word Search
- Pencils

Method:

Explore the many aspects of the Ascension through the use of a word search activity. This challenging game can help acquaint the children with the people, places, and themes associated with this event.

In advance, duplicate a copy of the "Words of Wonder" word search for each participant. Pass out the papers, and pencils, and ask the group to circle the words listed in the directions. As the children are working, or after they have completed the game, talk with them about the words and their significance to the Ascension story.

This activity may also be presented as a group project. Enlarge the word search and display it on a wall in the classroom. Invite the pupils to cooperate together to locate all of the items on the list. After the words have all been circled, read the Bible passage in unison to help the learners put them into context.

SYMBOLIC SNACKS

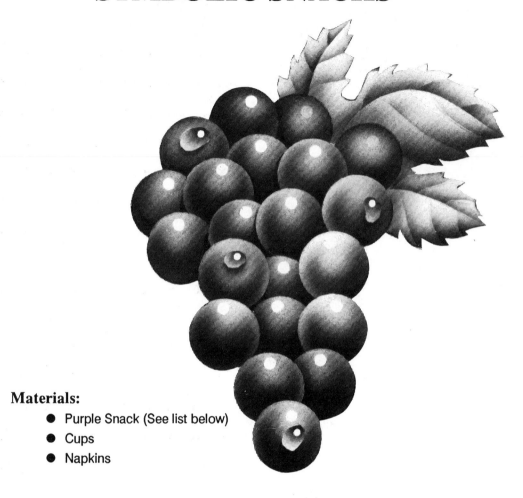

Materials:

- Purple Snack (See list below)
- Cups
- Napkins

Method:

Purple is a color which symbolizes royalty. It is an appropriate color to associate with the story of the Ascension, since the occasion was a royal event. After Jesus' work on earth was entrusted to the disciples, he ascended to heaven to rule at the right hand of God, his Father.

Introduce the concept of Jesus' royalty by serving a purple snack to the children. Some purple food and drink items include:

Grapes
Plums
Purple jello
Grape jelly
Plum jelly
Grape juice, drink or soda
Purple frosted cupcakes or cookies

Carry the theme even further by serving a snack on a purple tablecloth. Use plates, cups and napkins to match.

WE'RE AFIRE:
THE STORY OF PENTECOST

Scripture Passages: Acts 1 & 2

ROUND ROBIN REVIEW

Method:

When Peter and the other followers of Jesus gathered on the day of Pentecost, many amazing events took place. Review them with the children through the use of a cooperative method of storytelling called a Round Robin.

Gather the learners and ask them to sit in a circle. Explain that the group will be telling the story of Pentecost together and that each person will have an opportunity to add five words to it. Tell the participants that the collaborative account should include the following parts: the gathering on the day of Pentecost, the signs and symbols of the Holy Spirit's coming, the content of Peter's sermon and the way in which people were added to the church.

Begin the narrative for the group with five words, such as "On the Day of Pentecost." Go around the circle and provide an opportunity, as well as cues and encouragement, for each child to contribute to the story.

There are no supplies required for this activity, however, it may be helpful to have pictures or key words on cards to use to prompt the children during the Round Robin Review.

WONDER WINDSOCKS

Materials:

- Embroidery hoops, medium size
- White fabric, such as sheets, muslin, cotton
- Felt pieces, various colors
- Scissors
- Thread
- Needles
- Tacky glue
- String

Method:

Symbols such as tongues of fire, clouds, doves and wind are commonly associated with the story of Pentecost. A windsock decorated with some of these elements can illustrate the themes of this holy day and help the children remember the importance of it.

Pre-cut 1 yard by 22 inch pieces of white fabric for each participant and set them aside.

As a follow-up to telling the Pentecost story, have the children create symbols out of the felt pieces to illustrate the scripture passage. Ask each child to decide on one symbol to use for the project or up to four different ones. Place the felt, scissors, thread and needles within reach of the students. Instruct each person to cut four symbols out of the felt.

Hold up one of the large pieces of white fabric. Use the one yard portion as the length and the approximately two feet dimension as the width. Demonstrate how to sew the symbols onto the cloth. Place them in the top foot of the length, being certain to space the symbols two to three inches from each other.

Encourage the students to find a large space in which to work. Distribute the pre-cut fabric pieces, thread and needles. Tell the participants to thread their needles. Offer help to anyone who needs assistance. Guide the children as they position and sew their symbols to the material.

Provide scissors and show the pupils how to cut the lower two feet of their fabric pieces into two inch strips. These will form flowing streamers on the bottom of the windsocks.

Give each child a hoop and tell them to separate the two pieces. Pass out glue and teach the pupils how to affix the top edge of the windsock to the outer edge of the inner hoop. Using tacky glue will make this process easier. Provide two twelve inch pieces of string for each student. Tie them to the outer hoop to serve as the hanger for the windsock. Tell the learners to put their hoops back together and to tighten them. Allow the windsocks to dry for several hours before hanging them.

SPIRIT SYMBOLS

Materials:
- Paper plates, small size
- Plastic lids
- Paper cups
- Fabric scraps
- Yarn
- Markers or crayons
- Scissors
- Glue
- Hangers or hoops
- Paper punch
- Bible
- Poster listing the Fruits of the Spirit

Method:

Pentecost was a very special day for Jesus' followers. They were filled with the Spirit of their friend. Being filled and afire with the Holy Spirit empowered them to minister. They were blessed with many fruits of the Holy Spirit, which enabled them to accomplish great things. Today those who believe in Jesus are also given these fruits. Make mobiles to illustrate and teach the Fruits of the Spirit to the pupils in a creative way.

Set up a large table and display a variety of materials, such as small paper plates, plastic lids, yarn and trims, on it. Explain to the students that they will be making Fruit of the Spirit mobiles. Read Galatians 5:22 to the group and display the poster listing the nine fruits of the spirit. Talk and brainstorm with the students about the meaning of each Fruit. Associate symbols with the Fruits, such as heart for love, a smile for joy and the world for peace. Invite the children to use the provided materials to make their own symbols for each Fruit. The symbols may be cut, drawn, glued or town from or on the paper products, lids and fabric. Punch a hole in the top of each symbol. Cut nine pieces of yarn per person and help the children attach the yarn and symbol together. Pass out hoops or hangers to the boys and girls. Tell them to tie their Fruit symbols to the base of the mobile.

Suggest that the mobiles be hung in a window where the wind will add movement to the designs.

PENTECOST POETRY

Materials:

- Pencils or pens
- Paper or journal pages
- Crayons or markers

Method:

"The Holy Spirit descended upon them in tongues of fire and they were filled with astonishment." (Acts 2)

Jesus' followers must have shared many thoughts, feelings and words after they were filled with the power of the spirit in such a spectacular way.

Use Haiku, a Japanese form of poetry, consisting of three unrhymed lines, to help the learners write some of the thoughts and feelings that they associate with the Pentecost story. The first line contains five syllables, the second consists of seven syllables and the third line includes five syllables. The Fruits of the Spirit could be used as topics for the writing. They are love, joy, peace, patience, kindness, goodness, faithfulness, gentleness and self-control.

For example:

Pentecost a time
For breathing the Spirit wind
And dancing our life.

Spirit fill our life
With the fire of truth and love
For the kingdom now.

Gentleness, a gift
Given by the Spirit God
To help spread His peace.

Spirit gave us love
That we may share with all people
The gifts of the Son.

Once the poetry is written, invite the group to use crayons and markers to draw illustrations to highlight their Pentecost poems.

DRAMATIC DAY

Materials:
- Costume for Peter
- White sheet for Holy Spirit
- Construction paper, red and orange
- Scissors
- Fabric pieces for simple costumes
- Cassette tape; gusty, vibrant music
- Cassette player
- Fan

Method:

To be afire the Holy Spirit means to live in a special way. Peter tells us that we must repent and be baptized in the name of Jesus Christ in order to be filled with the Holy Spirit. A reenactment of the Pentecost event will help highlight the power of the Holy Spirit and the words of Peter.

Before the students arrive, use the red and orange construction paper to prepare a small flame of fire for each person.

Read Acts 2 aloud or play a tape of the story to the group. Talk with the children about the event and the words of Peter's sermon. Invite two volunteers to take the role of the Spirit and Peter while the rest of the class portrays the disciples and the followers. Provide the two volunteers with the appropriate costumes. Distribute fabric pieces to the rest of the students and help them drape and tie the material over their shoulders and heads.

Ask the volunteer playing the Holy Spirit to leave the room. Seat the children and Peter in a circle in a large open space. Once seated and quiet, have Peter stand and tell the group the message of Acts 1. This should include the selection of Matthais as a new apostle. Start the music and allow time for the participants to listen to it and to reflect on it. Turn on the fan to represent the wind and cue the person portraying the Holy Spirit to enter the space. Encourage the Spirit to dance about the room and the children distributing the pre-cut flames of fire to each follower. As he or she receives a flame, each follower should then get up and dance behind the Spirit. After a time, stop the wind and the music. Ask the children to sit down as the Spirit dances out of the room. Peter should share the message of Acts 2 and then exit the space.

Talk with the children about the experiences and any insights they may have learned or gained from this reinactment. Remind them that the flame of fire they were given is a sign that their lives continue to be filled with the same Spirit of Jesus.

SOUND SYMPHONY

Materials:
- Cassette Player
- Cassette tape, blank
- Materials for sound effects

Method:

Early on the day of Pentecost, a harvest feast, one hundred and twenty followers of Jesus gathered in a secret room to pray. They were waiting for power from God to help them go into the world to preach the Gospel. Suddenly, the room was filled with a sound, like mighty rushing wind, and soon the followers began to speak in different languages. The meeting room must have been filled with a symphony of sounds. Help the children experience this by creating a tape recording to represent these sounds.

After discussing the Pentecost story, ask each person to think of a sound he or she could make to represent the wind. Try to come up with as many different sounds as possible. This could include whistling, blowing and howling. It could also be simulated by rusting paper and turning on a fan. Pass around the tape recorder and allow time for each person to record the wind sound that was chosen. Play back the tape for the group.

Many languages were also heard on Pentecost. Choose a word, such as "Peace" and record it in different languages. Have each child pick a language and practice saying the word. Here are some suggestions:

French: Paix
Pronunciation: Peh

Russian: Mir
Pronunciation: Mere; rhymes with dear

Hungarian: Beke
Pronunciation: Bayh-kuh

Spanish: Paz
Pronunciation: Pah-th

Italian: Pace
Pronunciation: Pah-chay

Swahili: Amani
Pronunciation: Ah-mah-nee

Polish: Pokoj
Pronunciation: Poh-koy

Swedish, Danish and Norwegian: Fred
Pronunciation: Like man's name

Portuguese: Paz
Pronunciation: Rhymes with Roz

Vietnamese: Hoa-binh
Pronunciation: Hwa-bean

Take turns recording the words and play back the tape.

SINGING SESSION

Materials:

- Firewood
- Matches
- Music
- Guitar, optional

Method:

Tongues of fire were a tangible sign that the Holy Spirit had come. Creating a large bonfire in an outdoor area and holding a sing-a-long around it would help the children experience the story of this extraordinary day in a unique way.

Make a large bonfire and gather the children around it. Sing songs related to the theme of Pentecost. Some might include:

They'll Know We Are Christians by Love
Breathe on Me, Breathe of God
Spirit of the Living God
The Great Parade (Avery and Marsh)
Alleluia
Come, Holy Spirit
Dwell in Me, O Blessed Spirit
Creator, Spirit, by Whose Aid

It would be helpful to have someone accompany the singing with a guitar.

MEANINGFUL MEDITATION

Materials:
- Quiet background music
- Guided Meditation

Method:

The Season of Easter is filled with experiences and events in expectation of the coming of the Holy Spirit on the Day of Pentecost. Take time to pause to reflect on some of the thoughts and feelings associated with this event. Use this Meaningful Meditation to help the children prepare for the promised Paraclete. Play music, without words, quietly in the background. Read the meditation, with appropriate pauses, slowly and reflectively to the group.

Invite the students to close their eyes and to become very still. Tell them that they are going to go on a journey into their imagination. Encourage them to become aware of their own breath. Once the group is stilled, begin the guided meditation.

Guided Meditation:

In your mind's eye, you are leaving this room; this place. See yourself walking outside. It is an early morning in June. The blue sky overhead is full of white, fluffy clouds and the sun is warm on your face. You and a group of people are walking down an old, dusty road. You realize that it is no longer the twentieth century, but the time is 33 A.D. You notice that your clothes and the clothes of the people walking with you are flowing robes and that those who are not barefoot are wearing sandals.

You begin to walk faster as the group continues on. You feel that you are headed to a definite place, not exactly sure where that is. You begin to see a village at a distance up the road. The group of people are beginning to walk faster. You know in your heart that the place you are headed has something to do with your beloved friend, Jesus, who rose from the dead and has now ascended to heaven. You recall in your mind that before Jesus ascended to the Father he said he would send his Spirit to live among you and the world forever.

You are now standing in the village and a woman comes out of one of the houses and motions for you and the people to come in. You see yourself at a low table on the floor. The room becomes very still. The people around you all seem to be in deep prayer. You are aware of the smell of incense burning and the candles that are aflamed around the room. You, too, become very still.

In the flash of an instant, the room fills with a powerful wind and your whole being is moved by it. With great astonishment, you notice flames of fire above the heads of all those in the room. The people gathered begin to move about the room with great joy and dance. They are speaking to one another in languages different from their own. The presence and love of Jesus is abounding throughout the event. You realize that what is taking place is the sending of the Holy Spirit.

You and the people move from the room and begin to dance in the village. Many more people begin to follow and to become filled with the Spirit of Jesus. The group now begins its journey from the village down the dusty road. You are aware that as you return there is something wonderfully different about the way you feel. As you see yourself return to the twentieth century and to this place, open your eyes and be aware that you are filled with the Spirit, the power and the love of Jesus.

Invite the students to share their thoughts and feelings about their Pentecost journey.

CARTOON COMMUNICATION

Materials:
- Paper, 8 1/2" x 11"
- Paper cutter
- Markers

Method:

The early believers were afire with the Spirit and on the day of Pentecost three thousand people were added to the church. The children, as Jesus' followers are empowered by the Spirit and have the potential for spreading the Savior's story to many people. Create cartoon strips as a way to help the students think about ways they can witness of Jesus' love at home, school, in their community and other places.

In advance, cut the paper in half lengthwise. This will result in 4 1/4" x 11" strips. Distribute a piece, plus a marker, to each person. Instruct them to use the marker to divide the paper into four equal sections. Tell them that each section will be a frame of a cartoon strip. Ask the students to write the word "home" in the first square. Talk with them about ways in which they can demonstrate that they are afire with the Spirit at home. They can show love to siblings and parents in many ways. Ask them to draw a cartoon illustrating this theme in the first frame. Continue this process for the remaining three segments using words like church, school and community for the topics.

When the drawings are completed, it would be fun to assemble them as a cartoon page and let all the students "read" it.

PENTECOST PRAISE

Materials:

- Cassette tapes of music without words
- Cassette player
- Red fabric, pre-cut into 1 yard x 2 inch strips

Method:

When the promised Holy Spirit came on Pentecost, the disciples described it as like a rush of mighty wind. They saw flames of fire. They were able to speak to people from many different countries in foreign languages they had not studied. The great numbers who heard understood and became followers of Jesus.

Jesus said that his followers should be happy that he was going to heaven because then he could send his Spirit to live with the believers forever. This would be his link with them and the way he would continue to be with them and work through them.

Dance and movement are a fun way to express the wind-breath of the Holy Spirit. Talk with the children about the wind, which can be felt but not seen. Remind them of how wind dances through the trees and blows the leaves. Jesus said the Holy Spirit is like the wind. We hear and feel it, but we don't know where it comes from or where it goes.

Ask the students to stand in a line. Distribute a strip of red fabric to each of them. Tell them that they will be making a long cloth chain which will be used during the dance. Instruct the first person to tie the ends of his or her strip together to form the first fabric link. Direct the second student to add his or her strip to the first loop to begin the linked effect. Continue this procedure until all the strips have been connected and the chain is completed.

Space the students along the cloth chain and instruct them to hold onto it as they dance. Turn on the music and encourage the pupils to move to a rhythmic piece of music and to create the feeling of wind with their fabric chain. A suggested piece of music to use for this activity is the song "Storms of Africa" from the tape Watermark by Enya.

CREATIVE IDEAS FOR LENT

edited by Robert G. Davidson

After the successful response to **Creative Ideas for Advent,** we now offer a similar fine resource for Lent. In its more than one hundred pages, this book includes intergenerational events, worship ideas, activity projects, youth programs, lesson plans, stories, and many other ideas for use during the Lenten season.

The material is divided into three major sections—All Church Activities, Children's Activities, and Youth Activities. This does not mean that any of the material has to be limited to certain age groups. The possibilities are infinite of how you can use the ideas in this book.

Item: 2521 $12.95
ISBN 0-940754-25-8

CREATIVE IDEAS FOR LENT, Volume 2

edited by Robert and Linda Davidson

Due to the popularity of **Creative Ideas for Lent,** we have edited another seasonal resource. Here you will find more materials to make your Lenten programs truly memorable. Included in this volume you will find several plays, worship services, intergenerational events, crafts for children, study program ideas, meditations, puzzles and quizzes, youth programs, and much more.

In addition to the three regular sections—All Church Activities, Children's Activities, and Youth Activities—we have added a new one, Family Activities. We hope people will find material here to make the Easter event more meaningful to each member of the family.

Item: 2531 $12.95
ISBN 0-940754-62-2

ATTUNED TO GOD

by Elaine M. Ward

Lent is a time for listening and pondering, seeking and praying. Daily we encounter God in the ups and downs, ins and outs, silences and noises of life. Lent is the period when we hear again the story of God revealed in Christ, God's Word to us.

Some of these forty stories are Elaine Ward's own. Some are other people's stories, and from them, we hope, will come your story as you, too are attuned to God.

Item: 2653 $5.95
ISBN 0-940754-01-0

LENT:
THE SEASON OF SACRED STORIES

by Elaine M. Ward

"These stories are written..." so wrote the apostle John, telling the stories of Jesus, the Christ. Lent is the season we hear and tell "these stories," the stories that feed and sustain us.

Jesus is the parable of God and in Jesus' last story, coming to feed his disciples with the fish on the beach after the resurrection, he confronts Peter, and three times gives him the commission, "feed my sheep." As church educators who tell God's story during the blessed season of Lent, we "feed his sheep."

Elaine Ward, the storyteller, has given us another book of wonderful stories. Don't miss this new Lenten resource.

Item: 2657 $6.95
ISBN 0-940754-86-X

Order from:

EDUCATIONAL MINISTRIES, INC.

Call toll free: 800-221-0910